"Great harm
fered great l
have found o.. ...

—President George W. Bush

A Note from the Publisher

President George W. Bush's address to the nation
on September 20, 2001, has become one of those
speeches that even while you're listening to it, you
know will immediately impact the lives of hundreds of millions of people all over the world.
Politics bowed to leadership. The day after, *The
New York Times* described Congress's reception as
"a chamber transformed, partisanship melted
away in hugs across the aisle." Democratic minority leader, Representative Richard A. Gephardt,
said, "America speaks tonight with one voice."
Columnist Jay Ambrose said that the speech was
"as memorable in its language, meaning and style
of delivery as any given by a president in the mem-
ory of most Americans." And Gleaves Whitney,
Michigan Governor John Engler's chief speech
writer, wrote in the *Detroit News* that the speech
"has inspired our generation to be worthy of the
nation's founding and to leave something of last-
ing significance to our children."

Many worthy books will undoubtedly be written

about the events of September 11 and their after-math, and this speech will be part of those records. That's for the future. For now, as publishers, we believed people might want to have this little book as immediately as possible to put in their pockets or purse, to revisit the words that so strongly set our course as a nation in this crucial time. Most impor-tant, we all wanted to help raise funds to assist those affected by the tragedy. So we created this "instant book" as a donor channel, and we plan to publish it October 11, four weeks after the horrific day. In addition to the speech, we have provided a timeline of events.

Our profits from this book will go to the American Red Cross. Our first printing is 100,000 copies. Our fundraising effort is being supported by donations of services from our distributor, W. W. Norton & Company; manufacturers Bind-Rite Graphics, Bind-Rite Services, Jaguar Advanced Graphics, Offset Paperback Manufacturers, and City Diecutting; and designer Night & Day Design. With the help of these companies, volunteers and, most important, our dedicated Newmarket Press staff, we enlist your support and join you in praying for peace.

Esther Margolis, Publisher
New York City, October 2, 2001

★ COMMEMORATIVE EDITION ★

OUR MISSION
AND
OUR MOMENT

President George W. Bush's
ADDRESS TO THE NATION
Before a Joint Session of Congress
September 20, 2001

 Newmarket Press • New York

First Edition
10 9 8 7 6 5 4 3 2 1

ISBN 1-55704-523-2, single copy paperback

ISBN 1-55704-524-0, 24 copy carton

ISBN 1-55704-525-9, 100 copy carton

Library of Congress Catalog-in-Publication Data
is available upon request

QUANTITY PURCHASES
Companies, professional groups, clubs, and other organizations
may qualify for special terms when ordering quantities of this
title. For information, write Special Sales, Newmarket Press, 18
East 48th Street, New York, NY 10017, call (212) 832-3575,
fax (212) 832-3629, or e-mail mailbox@newmarketpress.com

www.newmarketpress.com

Manufactured in the United States of America

*Front cover illustration: President George W. Bush speaks before
the Joint Session of Congress, on September 20, 2001, to detail
his plan to combat terrorism. He holds the police badge of
George Howard, who died trying to save others at the World
Trade Center. Howard's badge was given to the President by
Howard's mother, Arlene. See page 23 for the President's refer-
ence in his speech. Photograph © 2001 by Corbis Sygma.*

*Back cover illustration: The World Trade Center with the Statue
of Liberty in the foreground, 1997. Photograph © 2001 by
Michael S. Yamashita/Corbis*

M r. Speaker, Mr. President
Pro Tempore, members of
Congress, and fellow Americans:

In the normal course of events, Presidents
come to this chamber to report on the
state of the Union. Tonight, no such
report is needed. It has already been
delivered by the American people.

We have seen it in the courage of passengers who rushed terrorists to save others
on the ground—passengers like an
exceptional man named Todd Beamer.
And would you please help me welcome
his wife, Lisa Beamer, here tonight.

We have seen the state of our Union in the endurance of rescuers, working past exhaustion. We've seen the unfurling of flags, the lighting of candles, the giving of blood, the saying of prayers—in English, Hebrew, and Arabic. We have seen the decency of a loving and giving people who have made the grief of strangers their own.

My fellow citizens, for the last nine days, the entire world has seen for itself the state of our Union, and it is strong.

Tonight, we are a country awakened to danger and called to defend freedom. Our grief has turned to anger and anger to resolution. Whether we bring our enemies to justice, or bring justice to our enemies, justice will be done.

I thank the Congress for its leadership at such an important time. All of America was touched on the evening of the tragedy to see Republicans and Democrats joined together on the steps of this Capitol, singing "God Bless America." And you did more than sing; you acted, by delivering $40 billion to rebuild our communities and meet the needs of our military.

Speaker Hastert, Minority Leader Gephardt, Majority Leader Daschle and Senator Lott, I thank you for your friendship, for your leadership and for your service to our country.

And on behalf of the American people, I thank the world for its outpouring of support. America will never forget the sounds of our National Anthem playing at Buckingham Palace, on the streets of Paris, and at Berlin's Brandenburg Gate.

We will not forget South Korean children gathering to pray outside our embassy in Seoul, or the prayers of sympathy offered at a mosque in Cairo. We will not forget moments of silence and days of mourning in Australia and Africa and Latin America.

Nor will we forget the citizens of 80 other nations who died with our own: dozens of Pakistanis; more than 130 Israelis; more than 250 citizens of India; men and women from El Salvador, Iran, Mexico and Japan; and hundreds of British citizens. America has no truer friend than Great Britain. Once again, we are joined together in a great cause— I'm so honored the British Prime Minister has crossed an ocean to show his unity of purpose with America. Thank you for coming, friend.

On September the 11th, enemies of freedom committed an act of war against our country. Americans have known wars—but for the past 136 years, they have been wars on foreign soil, except for one Sunday in 1941. Americans have known the casualties of war—but not at the center of a great city on a peaceful morning. Americans have known surprise attacks—but never before on thousands of civilians. All of this was brought upon us in a single day, and night fell on a different world—a world where freedom itself is under attack.

Americans have many questions tonight. Americans are asking: Who attacked our country? The evidence we have gathered all points to a collection of loosely affiliated terrorist organizations known as al Qaeda. They are some of the murderers indicted for bombing American embassies in Tanzania and Kenya, and responsible for bombing the USS *Cole*.

Al Qaeda is to terror what the mafia is to crime. But its goal is not making money; its goal is remaking the world—and imposing its radical beliefs on people everywhere.

The terrorists practice a fringe form of Islamic extremism that has been rejected by Muslim scholars and the vast majority of Muslim clerics—a fringe movement that perverts the peaceful teachings of Islam. The terrorists' directive commands them to kill Christians and Jews, to kill all Americans, and make no distinctions among military and civilians, including women and children.

This group and its leader—a person named Osama bin Laden—are linked to many other organizations in different countries, including the Egyptian Islamic Jihad and the Islamic Movement of Uzbekistan. There are thousands of these terrorists in more than 60 countries. They are recruited from their own nations and neighborhoods and brought to camps in places like Afghanistan, where they are trained in the tactics of terror. They are sent back to their homes or sent to hide in countries around the world to plot evil and destruction.

The leadership of al Qaeda has great influence in Afghanistan and supports the Taliban regime in controlling most of that country. In Afghanistan, we see al Qaeda's vision for the world.

Afghanistan's people have been brutal-ized—many are starving and many have fled. Women are not allowed to attend school. You can be jailed for owning a television. Religion can be practiced only as their leaders dictate. A man can be jailed in Afghanistan if his beard is not long enough.

The United States respects the people of Afghanistan—after all, we are currently its largest source of humanitarian aid—but we condemn the Taliban regime. It is not only repressing its own people, it is threatening people everywhere by sponsoring and sheltering and supplying terrorists. By aiding and abetting murder, the Taliban regime is committing murder.

And tonight the United States of America makes the following demands on the Taliban: Deliver to United States authorities all of the leaders of al Qaeda who hide in your land. Release all foreign nationals, including American citizens, you have unjustly imprisoned. Protect foreign journalists, diplomats and aid workers in your country. Close immediately and permanently every terrorist training camp in Afghanistan, and hand over every terrorist, and every person and their support structure, to appropriate authorities. Give the United States full access to terrorist training camps, so we can make sure they are no longer operating.

These demands are not open to negotiation or discussion. The Taliban must act, and act immediately. They will hand over the terrorists, or they will share in their fate.

I also want to speak tonight directly to Muslims throughout the world. We respect your faith. It's practiced freely by many millions of Americans, and by millions more in countries that America counts as friends. Its teachings are good and peaceful, and those who commit evil in the name of Allah blaspheme the name of Allah. The terrorists are traitors to their own faith, trying, in effect, to hijack Islam itself.

The enemy of America is not our many Muslim friends; it is not our many Arab friends. Our enemy is a radical network of terrorists, and every government that supports them.

Our war on terror begins with al Qaeda, but it does not end there. It will not end until every terrorist group of global reach has been found, stopped and defeated.

Americans are asking: Why do they hate us?

They hate what they see right here in this chamber—a democratically elected government. Their leaders are self-appointed. They hate our freedoms—our freedom of religion, our freedom of speech, our freedom to vote and assemble and disagree with each other.

They want to overthrow existing governments in many Muslim countries, such as Egypt, Saudi Arabia, and Jordan. They want to drive Israel out of the Middle East. They want to drive Christians and Jews out of vast regions of Asia and Africa.

These terrorists kill not merely to end lives, but to disrupt and end a way of life. With every atrocity, they hope that America grows fearful, retreating from the world and forsaking our friends. They stand against us, because we stand in their way.

We're not deceived by their pretenses to piety. We have seen their kind before.

They are the heirs of all the murderous ideologies of the 20th century. By sacrificing human life to serve their radical visions—by abandoning every value except the will to power—they follow in the path of fascism, and Nazism, and totalitarianism. And they will follow that path all the way, to where it ends: in history's unmarked grave of discarded lies.

Americans are asking: How will we fight and win this war? We will direct every resource at our command—every means of diplomacy, every tool of intelligence, every instrument of law enforcement, every financial influence and every necessary weapon of war—to the disruption and to the defeat of the global terror network.

This war will not be like the war against Iraq a decade ago, with a decisive liberation of territory and a swift conclusion.

It will not look like the air war above Kosovo two years ago, where no ground troops were used and not a single American was lost in combat.

Our response involves far more than instant retaliation and isolated strikes. Americans should not expect one battle, but a lengthy campaign, unlike any other we have ever seen. It may include dramatic strikes, visible on TV, and covert operations, secret even in success. We will starve terrorists of funding, turn them one against another, drive them from place to place, until there is no refuge or no rest. And we will pursue nations that provide aid or safe haven to terrorism. Every nation, in every region, now has a decision to make. Either you are with us, or you are with the terrorists. From this day forward, any nation that continues to harbor or support terrorism will be regarded by the United States as a hostile regime.

Our nation has been put on notice: We are not immune from attack. We will take defensive measures against terrorism to protect Americans. Today, dozens of federal departments and agencies, as well as state and local governments, have responsibilities affecting homeland security. These efforts must be coordinated at the highest level. So tonight I announce the creation of a Cabinet-level position reporting directly to me—the Office of Homeland Security.

And tonight, I also announce a distinguished American to lead this effort, to strengthen American security: a military veteran, an effective governor, a true patriot, a trusted friend—Pennsylvania's Tom Ridge.

He will lead, oversee and coordinate a comprehensive national strategy to safeguard our country against terrorism, and respond to any attacks that may come.

These measures are essential. But the only way to defeat terrorism as a threat to our way of life is to stop it, eliminate it, and destroy it where it grows.

Many will be involved in this effort, from FBI agents to intelligence operatives to the reservists we have called to active duty. All deserve our thanks, and all have our prayers. And tonight, a few miles from the damaged Pentagon, I have a message for our military: Be ready. I've called the armed forces to alert, and there is a reason. The hour is coming when America will act, and you will make us proud.

This is not, however, just America's
fight. And what is at stake is not just
America's freedom. This is the world's
fight. This is civilization's fight. This is
the fight of all who believe in progress
and pluralism, tolerance and freedom.

We ask every nation to join us. We will
ask, and we will need, the help of police
forces, intelligence services, and banking
systems around the world. The United
States is grateful that many nations and
many international organizations have
already responded—with sympathy and
with support. Nations from Latin
America, to Asia, to Africa, to Europe, to
the Islamic world. Perhaps the NATO
Charter reflects best the attitude of the
world: An attack on one is an attack on
all.

The civilized world is rallying to
America's side. They understand that if

this terror goes unpunished, their own cities, their own citizens may be next. Terror, unanswered, cannot only bring down buildings, it can threaten the stability of legitimate governments. And you know what? We're not going to allow it. Americans are asking: What is expected of us? I ask you to live your lives and hug your children. I know many citizens have fears tonight, and I ask you to be calm and resolute, even in the face of a continuing threat.

I ask you to uphold the values of America and remember why so many have come here. We are in a fight for our principles, and our first responsibility is to live by them. No one should be singled out for unfair treatment or unkind words because of their ethnic background or religious faith.

I ask you to continue to support the victims of this tragedy with your contributions. Those who want to give can go to a central source of information, libertyunites.org, to find the names of groups providing direct help in New York, Pennsylvania, and Virginia.

The thousands of FBI agents who are now at work in this investigation may need your cooperation, and I ask you to give it.

I ask for your patience with the delays and inconveniences that may accompany tighter security and for your patience in what will be a long struggle.

I ask your continued participation and confidence in the American economy. Terrorists attacked a symbol of American prosperity. They did not touch its source. America is successful because of

the hard work, and creativity, and enter-
prise of our people. These were the true
strengths of our economy before
September 11th, and they are our
strengths today.

And finally, please continue praying for
the victims of terror and their families,
for those in uniform, and for our great
country. Prayer has comforted us in
sorrow, and will help strengthen us for
the journey ahead.

Tonight I thank my fellow Americans for
what you have already done and for
what you will do. And ladies and gen-
tlemen of the Congress, I thank you,
their representatives, for what you have
already done and for what we will do
together.

Tonight, we face new and sudden
national challenges. We will come

together to improve air safety, to dramatically expand the number of air marshals on domestic flights, and take new measures to prevent hijacking. We will come together to promote stability and keep our airlines flying, with direct assistance during this emergency.

We will come together to give law enforcement the additional tools it needs to track down terror here at home. We will come together to strengthen our intelligence capabilities to know the plans of terrorists before they act, and find them before they strike.

We will come together to take active steps that strengthen America's economy, and put our people back to work.

Tonight, we welcome two leaders who embody the extraordinary spirit of all New Yorkers: Governor George Pataki and Mayor Rudolph Giuliani. As a symbol of America's resolve, my administration will work with Congress, and these two leaders, to show the world that we will rebuild New York City.

After all that has just passed—all the lives taken, and all the possibilities and hopes that died with them—it is natural to wonder if America's future is one of fear. Some speak of an age of terror. I know there are struggles ahead, and dangers to face. But this country will define our times, not be defined by them. As long as the United States of America is determined and strong, this will not be an age of terror; this will be an age of liberty, here and across the world.

Great harm has been done to us. We have suffered great loss. And in our grief and anger we have found our mission and our moment. Freedom and fear are

21

at war. The advance of human freedom—the great achievement of our time, and the great hope of every time—now depends on us. Our nation—this generation—will lift the dark threat of violence from our people and our future. We will rally the world to this cause by our efforts, by our courage. We will not tire, we will not falter, and we will not fail.

It is my hope that in the months and years ahead, life will return almost to normal. We'll go back to our lives and routines, and that is good. Even grief recedes with time and grace. But our resolve must not pass. Each of us will remember what happened that day, and to whom it happened. We will remember the moment the news came—where we were and what we were doing. Some will remember an image of a fire, or a story of rescue. Some will carry memories of a face and a voice gone forever.

And I will carry this: It is the police shield of a man named George Howard, who died at the World Trade Center trying to save others. It was given to me by his mom, Arlene, as a proud memorial to her son. This is my reminder of lives that ended, and a task that does not end.

I will not forget the wound to our country and those who inflicted it. I will not yield; I will not rest; I will not relent in waging this struggle for freedom and security for the American people.

The course of this conflict is not known, yet its outcome is certain. Freedom and fear, justice and cruelty, have always been at war, and we know that God is not neutral between them.

Fellow citizens, we'll meet violence with patient justice—assured of the rightness of our cause, and confident of the victories to come.

In all that lies before us, may God grant us wisdom, and may he watch over the United States of America.

Thank you.

TIMELINE OF EVENTS
September 11–September 20, 2001

(All times Eastern Daylight Time)

9/11/2001 (Tuesday)

7:59AM American Airlines Flight 11 departs
Boston's Logan International Airport,
bound for Los Angeles. Aboard are 81
passengers and 11 crew.

8:01AM United Airlines Flight 93 leaves
Newark, New Jersey for San Francisco,
with 45 people on board.

8:10AM American Airlines Flight 77 takes off
from Dulles International Airport in
Washington, DC, heading for Los
Angeles. Sixty-four passengers and crew
are on board.

8:14AM United Airlines Flight 175 leaves
Boston, bound for Los Angeles, with
56 passengers and 9 crew aboard.

Each of the four planes is taken over by at least three hijackers, who were reportedly armed with knives and box cutters.

8:45AM American Airlines Flight 11, a Boeing 767, crashes into the north tower of the World Trade Center in New York City, tearing into the side of the building at about the 100th floor and setting it on fire. A thick dust cloud billows from the tower's upper floors.

9:03AM A huge fireball erupts as United Airlines Flight 175, a Boeing 767, slams into the south tower of the World Trade Center, exploding at about the 90th floor.

9:05AM President George W. Bush, at an elementary school in Sarasota, Florida, is informed of the attacks.

9:17AM The Federal Aviation Administration shuts down New York City airports.

9:21AM The Port Authority closes all New York City bridges and tunnels.

Timeline of Events

9:30AM Trading is suspended as the New York
Stock Exchange is evacuated.

President Bush, in Florida, calls the
plane crashes "an apparent terrorist
attack" and orders a "full-scale investigation."

9:40AM For the first time in U.S. history, the
FAA stops all commercial air traffic
nationwide, canceling flights and forc-
ing all airborne planes to land.

9:43AM Washington, DC: American Airlines
Flight 77, a Boeing 757, crashes into
the west side of the Pentagon, U.S. military intelligence headquarters, hitting
at the second floor.

9:45AM The White House is evacuated.

10:05AM The south tower of the World Trade
Center, an 110-story building, suddenly
collapses, sending up an enormous
cloud of dust, debris, and smoke.

10:10AM Part of the Pentagon collapses.

United Airlines Flight 93, a Boeing 747, crashes in Somerset County, Pennsylvania (southeast of Pittsburgh). Later, authorities believe the flight may have been headed for the White House, Camp David, or the Capitol, and reports based on cell phone calls from the plane prior to the crash indicate that passengers may have thwarted the hijackers.

10:28AM The north tower of the World Trade Center, also 110-stories, collapses from the top down, erupting into massive clouds of smoke and debris. Downtown Manhattan is blanketed in dust.

10:30AM New York Governor George Pataki declares a state of emergency.

11:02AM New York City mayor Rudolph Giuliani orders the area south of Canal Street in Manhattan evacuated.

11:18AM American Airlines and United Airlines confirm the plane crashes. There are no survivors.

12:04AM Los Angeles International Airport is evacuated.

12:15PM San Francisco International Airport is evacuated.

The U.S. closes its Canada and Mexico borders.

1:04PM President Bush, speaking from Barksdale Air Force Base in Shreveport, Louisiana, says the U.S. military is on high alert around the world and promises the U.S. will "hunt down and punish those responsible" for the attacks.

1:27PM A state of emergency is declared in Washington, DC by mayor Anthony Williams.

1:48PM President Bush, aboard Air Force One, flies to Offutt Air Force Base near Omaha, Nebraska.

4:10PM Building 7 of the World Trade Center, damaged by the earlier collapses, is on fire.

4:30PM The president leaves Nebraska to return to Washington.

5:20PM Building 7 of the World Trade Center, 47 stories tall, collapses.

6:00PM Explosions occur in Kabul, Afghanistan (2:30AM local time), the country harboring Osama bin Laden who officials believe is behind the terrorist attacks. The U.S. was not involved in the Kabul explosions, which were attributed to the Northern Alliance (a group fighting Afghanistan's Taliban regime).

6:54PM President Bush arrives at the White House.

8:30PM The president addresses the nation, asking for prayers for the victims and their families, and promising that the United States will make no distinction between those who committed the terrorist acts and the governments who harbor them.

9/12/01 (Wednesday)

10:30AM New York Mayor Rudolph Giuliani
         announces that the death count will be
         in the thousands.

10:50AM President Bush declares that the attacks
         are an "act of war."

11:25AM Three police officers and six firefight-
         ers are rescued from the debris of the
         World Trade Center.

1:00PM   In Boston, Massachusetts, and Florida
         the FBI takes several people into cus-
         tody for questioning.

2:57PM   The White House has evidence that the
         White House and Air Force One were
         targets in the attacks.

4:40PM   It is revealed by U.S. Attorney General
         John Ashcroft that several of the sus-
         pected hijackers attended pilot training
         the United States. He announces that
         the aircrafts were hijacked by between
         three and six people, who were
         equipped with box cutters and knives.

TIMELINE OF EVENTS

4:50PM It is revealed that Nasdaq and the New York Stock Exchange will not open before Friday.

5:45PM Relatives of Jeremy Glick, a victim of the Pennsylvania plane crash, say they received a mobile phone call from him saying the passengers on board tried to overtake the hijackers. Shortly after, the plane crashed.

11:04PM Police say they have arrested a man with phony identity papers at Kennedy airport. Nine more men have been in detained.

11:50PM The FBI issues search warrants for addresses in Florida in their hunt for the perpetrators.

9/13/01 (Thursday)

Morning: President George Bush and First Lady Laura Bush visit the Washington Hospital Center, where they see 11 military and civilian workers from the Pentagon.

32

Rescue crews search for survivors. Ninety-four people are confirmed dead. 4,763 individuals have been reported missing.

At the Pentagon, the fire is extinguished and rescue workers search for more survivors. It is estimated that about 190 individuals, including the passengers aboard the airplane, died in the attack.

The New York Stock Exchange, Nasdaq Stock Market, and other financial markets are closed for a third day.

Afternoon: Two firemen, who had fallen into a crevice, are rescued from the rubble.

The flight data recorder from the Pentagon crash is recovered. Initial reports suggest that it is blank.

1:50PM There are reports as many as 50 people could have been behind the terrorist attacks.

5:13PM In Pennsylvania, the flight data recorder from United Flight 93 has been found.

6:40PM U.S. Vice President Dick Cheney goes to the Camp David presidential retreat as a safety measure. President George Bush stays at the White House.

10:53PM Philippine authorities detained suspected foreign bombers and are investigating the possibility of their connection to the terrorist attacks.

9/14/01 (Friday)

Morning: Airports across the country begin to reopen, as well as New York's three major airports. The FAA announces Boston's Logan International won't reopen until safety measures are stricter.

12:00PM At the National Cathedral, a National Day of Remembrance is held. President Bush and four former presidents—Bill Clinton, George H.W. Bush, Jimmy

Carter, and Gerald Ford lead the nation in prayer.

Afternoon & Evening: The FBI identifies 18 individuals as the hijackers, and Secretary of State Colin Powell announces that Osama bin Laden is the prime suspect in the attacks.

The National Football League cancels its weekend games. College football is also postponed.

9/15/01 (Saturday)

President Bush receives authorization from the U.S. Senate to use military force against the terrorists. The Senate grants $40 billion in emergency spending.

President Bush authorizes calling up 35,500 reservists.

President Bush visits New York to assess the damage and give moral support to residents.

In Kabul, Taliban leaders say they expect the U.S. to attack and vow to seek revenge.

Airspace in the United States is reopened to foreign airlines.

Afghanistan threatens Pakistan and other surround countries with invasion if the United States is allowed to use their airspace or military.

Continental Airlines lays off 12,000 employees.

The first of the New York victims are given funerals.

9/16/01 (Sunday)

Victims of the attack are remembered in memorial services across the country.

Vice President Dick Cheney asks American investors to buy stocks when the stock markets reopen on Monday.

A delegation sent by Pakistan meets with the Taliban regarding the hand-over of Osama bin Laden.

9/17/01 (Monday)

Morning: Stock markets open. The Dow drops 684.81 points and closes below 9,000 Nasdaq falls more than 115 points to 1,579.55.

Family and friends of victims on board United Flight 93 hold a memorial service, in which First Lady Laura Bush attends.

U.S. Airways declares it will cut flights and lay off 11,000 employees.

The Taliban discusses their conditions for possibly deporting Osama bin Laden to a country other than the United States.

Evening: Attorney General John Ashcroft announces that the FBI is investigating 47,000 leads, and has taken 49 individuals for questioning. He declares they are still looking for 200 others.

President Bush visits the Washington Islamic Center and condemns acts of prejudice and violence against Arab Americans and Muslims.

Major League baseball continues.

9/18/01 Tuesday

After the Pakistani delegation leaves, the Taliban says it needs proof that Osama bin Laden was behind the attack before they will turn him over.

Financial officials examine whether Osama bin Laden tried to financially benefit from the attacks.

Airlines request government bailout and takeover of insurance liability on attack claims.

9/19/01 (Wednesday)

Stocks continue to drop, as economic officials discuss how to reinforce the economy.

More bodies are recovered from the rubble in New York.

Boeing Airlines prepares to lay off 30,000 employees.

The United Nations cancels its annual meeting in New York.

9/20/01 (Thursday)

President Bush requests $5 billion from Congress for an airline bailout, as well as to help with any lawsuits the airlines are facing.

Osama bin Laden is asked to leave Afghanistan by Islamic clerics.

Great Britain and the United States build up their military presence in the Persian Gulf.

President Bush addresses the nation from the United States Capitol and demands that Afghanistan hand over Osama bin Laden.

Two weeks after the September 11th attack, the number of dead and missing at the World Trade Center in New York City is 6,412. Another 184 people perished at the Pentagon in a similar attack, and 41 more died when a hijacked plane crashed in the Pennsylvania countryside. The total number of people presumed dead is 6,637.

Acknowledgments

Newmarket Press thanks the following people and companies who provided immediate and generous cooperation, support, and donations of services and goods to make this fundraising effort as effective as possible:

The executives, sales, distribution, and warehouse staff of W. W. Norton & Company, especially Drake McFeeley, Bill Rusin, and Dosier Hammond, for contributing services and support; Bind-Rite Graphics and Bind-Rite Services in New Jersey for donating the first printing, especially Andy Merson, John Sposato, Helder Gomes, Lou DeRosa, Alan Merson, and Elliot Ward; Bradley Corrugated Box Company in New Jersey for donating the cartons; Offset Paperback Manufacturers in Pennsylvania for donating additional printings, especially Joe Makarewicz; Jaguar Advanced Graphics in New York for donating the cover printing, especially Vincent Severino, Linda Wallace, and Dave Goldberg; City Diecutting Inc. in New Jersey for donating packaging, especially Eric De Vos; Night & Day Design, especially Tim Shaner, for creating time where there was none to design the cover, and Chris Measom for his support.

Thanks also to publishing colleagues Michael Murphy, Maureen Golden, Rena Wolner, and Sally Anne McCartin, who volunteered valuable time and advice; Barbara Kipper Levy, Howard Reese, and Marianne Nemetz of Levy Book Company in Chicago, whose early commitment was most helpful; my husband, Dr. Stanley Fisher, for support, as always; and most of all, I am grateful to the staff of compassionate professionals with whom I am fortunate to work. Their commitment made this effort possible: The editorial and production team led by Keith Hollaman and Frank DeMaio, with vital support from Tom Perry, Michelle Howry, Julia Moberg, and Kathryn McHugh; our marketing and publishing group Ellen Simon, Harry Burton, Leslie Rowe, Corey Onaro, Yulia Borodyanskaya, Kelli Taylor, Ann Lee, Meredith Hirsch, Harry Bevans; and Maina Lopotukhin.

Lastly, a dedication to Robert Mayo, one of the missing at the World Trade Center and brother-in-law of valued Newmarket colleague Tracey Bussell. Employed as a Fire Safety Director in the lobby of Tower #4, Robert stayed on his job to help others to safety. His last phone call to his wife Meryl was at 9:20AM, saying he was leaving to join his supervisor and three other associates to further aid the rescue effort. None of the five survived. When his eleven-year-old son, Corbin, asks his mother why his father didn't just leave when he could have, Meryl responds, "He was doing his job . . . he was a hero." Our heartfelt condolences to the Mayo and Bussell families.

—Esther Margolis, President and Publisher,
Newmarket Press